GOD'S DEVIL

The Incredible Story of How Satan's
Rebellion Serves God's Purpose

STUDY GUIDE

ERWIN W. LUTZER

MOODY PUBLISHERS
CHICAGO

Scripture quotations are from the ESV® Bible (The Holy Bible, English Standard Ver-
sion®), copyright © 2001 by Crossway, a publishing ministry of Good News Publishers.
Used by permission. All rights reserved.

Developed by Dana Gould
Cover design: Smartt Guys design
Interior design: Erik M. Peterson
Cover image: The Archangel Michael strikes Lucifer, Pitati, Bonifazio de' (1487-1553) / Santi
         Giovanni e Paolo, Venice, Italy / Cameraphoto Arte Venezia / Bridgeman Images

ISBN: 978-0-8024-1315-4

We hope you enjoy this book from Moody Publishers. Our goal is to provide high-quality,
thought-provoking books and products that connect truth to your real needs and challenges. For more information on other books and products written and produced from a
biblical perspective, go to www. moodypublishers.com or write to:

Moody Publishers
820 N. LaSalle Boulevard
Chicago, IL 60610

3 5 7 9 10 8 6 4

Printed in the United States of America

CONTENTS

God's Devil, Chapter 1:
PUTTING THE DEVIL IN HIS PLACE

A Summary from the Book

This book is a modest attempt to put the devil in his place. When Lucifer (whose name means "light bearer") rolled the dice, gambling that he could do better by being God's enemy rather than God's friend, he set in motion a moral catastrophe that would reverberate throughout the universe. You and I have been deeply affected by his decision made in the ages long ago.

Any power Lucifer would exercise would always be subject to God's will and decree. Thus moment by moment he would suffer the humiliation of knowing that he could never be the ultimate cause of his existence and power.

We need to be reminded of Martin Luther's words that

even the "devil is God's devil." We have forgotten that only when we know who God is can we know who the devil is. Blessed are those who are convinced that the prince of this world has become the slave of the Prince of Peace.

This book attempts to give an overview of the career of Satan and his interaction with the Almighty. It traces his fall from an exalted position to his defeat by Christ and to his demise in everlasting shame and contempt. It attempts to prove that Satan always loses even when he "wins." Best of all, it shows that we who have been translated from the kingdom of darkness into the kingdom of light are able to stand against him.

My first premise is that God has *absolute sovereignty in His universe.* That means that even evil is a part of the larger plan of God. Of course, I do not mean to imply that God either does evil or approves of it. However, I do mean that by virtue of His roles as Creator and sustainer of the universe, God is the ultimate (though not the immediate) cause of all that comes to pass.

My second premise is that God *uses our conflict with Satan to develop character.* These struggles give us the opportunity to have our faith tested. Our spiritual war is a classroom where we can learn about the deceitfulness of sin and the chastisement of God—along with His grace and power.

I am convinced that unless we grasp how the devil fits into God's scheme of things, we will find it more difficult to stand against his conspiracy against us personally and his influence within our culture. How we perceive our enemy will largely determine how we fight against him.

ENGAGING THE TOPIC

Complete the statements below after reading the book and the above summary. Then, during your class or small-group meeting, watch the DVD, Session 1.

1. Satan was defeated the moment he chose to _____.

2. The portrait of Satan, which dominated much of medieval thinking, was not based on the Bible but on popular _____.

3. At the _____, Lucifer was defeated spiritually.

4. When Satan is thrown into the lake of fire, he will be defeated _____.

5. God uses our conflict with Satan to develop our _____.

6. The biblical portrait of Satan is that he indeed does have great power, but that it is always limited by the _____ and _____ of God.

QUESTIONS FOR DISCUSSION

1. Discuss the author's statement that "God has absolute sovereignty in His universe." What does that tell us? How do we reconcile that with the evil we see in the world today?

2. Satan has already been defeated *strategically*. What was the decisive factor in his defeat? What prevailing conditions must Satan endure as a result of his defeat?

3. What ensured Satan's defeat *spiritually*? In what ways does his spiritual defeat impact him?

4. What will Satan's eternal punishment involve? (See Revelation 20:14.)

5. Dante's classic, *Inferno*, gives a portrait of Satan that dominated much of medieval thinking. Describe the details of his view of Satan. Why is Dante's view erroneous?

6. In his poems *Paradise Lost* and *Paradise Regained,* how did Milton portray Lucifer? What helpful contributions did Milton make to his readers' general understanding of Satan? Where did Milton fall short in his portrayal?

7. Discuss Goethe's devil, Mephistopheles. How does Goethe distort scriptural teaching about the devil? In what ways can we see his devil fitting within the framework of contemporary America?

8. The author mentions a poll that indicates that at least 25 percent of Americans believe that the devil is only a symbol of man's inhumanity to man. Of those who believe in the devil, only a small percentage believe they have ever been tempted by him. What does that tell us about the "spiritual temperature" of our country? How do you respond to family, friends, and coworkers who share those beliefs?

9. One of Dr. Lutzer's premises in this chapter is that God uses our conflict with Satan to develop character. As believers, what do we gain from our conflict with such a powerful, evil being?

10. The theme of our study is spiritual warfare. Against Satan and his army, we are battling a powerful enemy. What makes us confident we are in a winnable war?

Scripture teaches us that Christ's sacrifice on the cross defeated Satan and his purpose of destroying the entire human race (John 12:31–34). Although Satan has great power, it is always limited by the purposes and plans of God. Believers are under constant attack by the enemy, as Satan is engaged in a great war with God for the souls of men and women. But we walk by faith victoriously, for it is the resurrected Christ who intercedes for us to the right hand of God (Romans 8:34). When we do sin, Satan will accuse us before God. But by God's grace, if we confess our sins, we are forgiven and cleansed by the blood of Christ (1 John 1:9; 2:1;

Hebrews 13:20–21).

James 4:7 tells us, "Submit yourselves therefore to God. Resist the devil, and he will flee from you." The key to resisting the devil is to first submit to God. The word "resist" in the Greek text here is the word *anthistemi*, which means "take a stand against." When we stand against the devil and his underlings, we do so in the name and authority of Jesus Christ. To be effective, however, we must equip ourselves by putting on the full armor of God (Ephesians 6:11–18).

All God's people experience personal struggles with the enemy. When we face temptation, let us remember that Jesus, when tempted by Satan, used Scripture to rebuke him. Read Matthew 4:1–10, where Satan tempted Jesus three times. In all three cases, Jesus used Scripture to resist Satan and defeat him. We too can defeat Satan by properly using the Word of God.

Take time to daily engage God's Word:

- Spend time getting know God's Word. Ask God to help you apply it to your life.

- Memorize God's Word. "Store" God's truth in your heart and mind.

- Meditate on God's Word. Feed your soul with its truths (Psalm 1:2).

- Use God's Word when facing temptation. The Holy Spirit will enable you to use God's Word in your battles against the devil.

Always remember that the Holy Spirit within us helps teach the truth of God's Word. "But the Helper, the Holy Spirit, whom the Father will send in my name, he will teach you all things and bring to your remembrance all that I have said to you" (John 14:26).

ENGAGING THE TOPIC answers:

1. sin   2. folklore   3. cross   4. eternally   5. character
6. purposes, plans

God's Devil, Chapter 2:

THE STAR THAT BIT THE DUST

A Summary from the Book

You were in Eden, the garden of God." With this single statement, we enter into a world that lies just beyond our imagination. It is a world of beauty, peace, and unity. It is a world so unlike what we've experienced that it strains the limits of our fancy. To see the gardens in the Schonbrunn palace of Vienna is wonder enough; just imagine the "garden of God"!

Yet here in a realm beyond our grasp, a glorious creature chose to take cosmic gamble that would backfire. He tripped a series of dominoes whose interrelationships were unknown to him. His act, once accomplished, would reverberate for all of eternity; the entire universe would shudder, reeling from the shock. Even now, you and I feel the painful effects.

The Bible invites us to part the curtain, to glimpse the whys and wherefores of Lucifer's rebellion. Two prophets of the Old Testament tell the story of a being who is more than simply a human king; they introduce us to that world where the grand, cosmic gamble was made. Both Isaiah and Ezekiel tell the same story, but from slightly different points of view.

Why would a perfect creature become dissatisfied in a perfect world? This was a being who evidently was fulfilled in serving God; if he was satisfied, why rebel? We do know that Lucifer was deceived, thinking that rebellion was necessary if he were to put his own interests first. He failed to grasp that even if he were motivated by self-interest, obedience to God would still be best.

Lucifer would now learn what all creatures must: We might be able to control our decisions, but we cannot control the results. *Sin triggers the law of unintended consequences.*

Lucifer's bad judgment is a warning to us. We must never think that our obedience is best for God, but not best for us. When God commands us to obey Him, He not only has His best interests in mind but ours too. That is why we are never wiser than when we choose to follow God's will, whatever the cost.

ENGAGING THE TOPIC

Complete the statements below after reading the book and the above summary. Then, during your class or small-group meeting, watch the DVD, Session 2.

1. The _____ our God, the _____ our devil.

2. Any created creature would of necessity fall short of the limitless *perfect* of the Almighty.

3. No decision is this life can ever be good unless it is good for *eternity*

4. With regard to Satan's fall, Frances Thompson said, "Satan will never again *Sing* but only *howl*"

5. Although Lucifer is _____, he is not _____.

6. _____ caused Satan to gamble his privileges away.

QUESTIONS FOR DISCUSSION

1. Read Ezekiel 28:15–17. From that passage, what can we conclude was Lucifer's base sin?

2. In Ezekiel 28:15 we find a theological puzzle. God tells Lucifer that "unrighteousness was found in you." Prior to that, Lucifer had been a righteous being. How can an unrighteous choice arise out of a righteous being?

3. Drawing from passages in Isaiah and Exodus, Dr. Lutzer mentions five goals that have motivated Lucifer's arrogant actions. Discuss each of Lucifer's "I will" passages. After interacting with those Scripture texts, how might you assess Lucifer's thoughts and actions?

4. Lucifer wanted to be "like the Most High." Although he was a creature of limitations, he tried to mimic all of God's perfections such as His omnipresence and His omnipotence. How many of those could Lucifer have hoped to achieve?

5. Although Lucifer knew God, how was his understanding of God limited? Upon what was his misunderstanding based?

6. In his discussion of the difference between time and eternity, Dr. Lutzer provides a lesson for us: "No decision can be considered good if eternity proves it to be bad." How did that lesson apply to Lucifer? How might it apply to us?

7. Satan's gamble failed because he miscalculated the consequences of his sin. In what ways do we miscalculate the consequences of our sin? What was the result of our miscalculations?

8. One-third of the angels in heaven rebelled and joined with Lucifer. Read 1 Timothy 5:21. What can we conclude from this Scripture passage regarding their fall?

9. When God responded to Lucifer's rebellion, He could have simply annihilated Lucifer, but He did not. Instead, what course of action did God take, and why?

10. God laid out three rules for engaging the conflict with Satan. Discuss each rule, the purpose for each, and what each demonstrated.

PERSONAL REFLECTION

Lucifer's bad judgment is a warning to us. We must never think that our obedience is best for God, but not best for us. When God commands us to obey Him, He not only has His best interests in mind but ours too. That is why we are never wiser than when we choose to follow God's will, whatever the cost.

Lucifer learned what all creatures must: We might be able to control our decisions, but we cannot control the results. Sin triggers the law of unintended results. In Lucifer's case, pride caused him to gamble his privileges away. He had underestimated God and overestimated himself. No decision is this life can ever be good unless it is good for eternity. When we are tempted to give in to sin, the devil never advertises the negative consequences of a disobedient action. All of us face countless decisions every day. We must ask God to guide us, especially when temptation can have a critical impact on our decision making. Let us begin each day by taking to heart these verses: "Trust in the Lord with all your heart, and do not lean on your own understanding. In all your ways acknowledge him, and he will make straight your paths. Be not wise in your own eyes; fear the Lord, and turn away from evil" (Proverbs 3:5–7).

We have learned that God will not compromise His own holiness and justice. As He has shown with Lucifer, He does not only win with power, but by righteousness. The battle is not determined by who is the strongest, but who is right and just. We are all born with a drop of Lucifer's rebellion in our hearts. We stand, as it were, between him and God, in the crossfire. Whether we choose the winner or loser will determine our destiny. For we get to spend eternity with the God we love and serve.

ENGAGING THE TOPIC answers:

1. greater, smaller   2. perfections   3. eternity
4. sing, howl   5. intelligent, wise   6. Pride

God's Devil, Chapter 3:

THERE IS A SERPENT IN OUR GARDEN

A Summary from the Book

Satan ignored all the warning bells. Even after his fall, clear thinking should have assured him that greater disobedience would only result in greater torment. Though his doom in hell was sealed the moment he sinned, if he were to withdraw from the battle, his torments would have been more tolerable. But in his foolishness, the thrill of winning a battle today only postponed a greater pain in the lake of fire tomorrow. And thus we have evil exposed for what it is: The desire to oppose God even with the full knowledge that in the end the Almighty will triumph.

Far from withdrawing, Satan chose to escalate the conflict. Admitting defeat was too humbling; better to forge ahead with sustained rebellion than withdraw from the fray and accept his punishment. He would pretend that illusion is reality; he would call his defeats triumphs. And he would store up more retribution by expanding his rebellious rule.

As we have learned, other angels followed him. Whether motivated by loyalty or by a craving for their own power and independence, some chose to participate in the great gamble. How many angels followed Satan? If it was a third of the angelic realm, the number of rebels might have been in the hundreds of millions.

Satan's next target was human beings. They were made in God's image and had a capacity for fellowship with God that not even the angels possessed. If Adam and Eve were to sin, they would not only contaminate themselves but their offspring. Satan waited for the right moment to make his move. This was an opportunity he would not miss!

Here we have our first glimpse into the satanic mind and begin to see how this fallen angel operates. As Christ taught, "He is a liar and the father of lies" (John 8:44).

ENGAGING THE TOPIC

Complete the statements below after reading the book and the above summary. Then, during your class or small-group meeting, watch the DVD, Session 3.

1. Every time we sin, we affirm the original _____ of Eden.

2. Confusing the voice of _____ and the voice of the _____ is not difficult.

3. Whatever restrictions God gives us are for our
   _____ and not our _____.

4. _____ began the moment Adam and Eve ate the
   fruit.

5. Adam and Eve died _____ in that they were separated from God. They would also die _____ unless
   God were to intervene.

6. Satan lies about himself, making himself to appear
   _____.

7. In order to lure man away from God, the serpent
   planted the seeds of *Cult* religion.

QUESTIONS FOR DISCUSSION

1. Revelation 5:11 tells us that in heaven there are "many
   angels, numbering myriads of myriads and thousands of
   thousands." The Bible tells that one-third of the angelic
   realm followed Satan (Revelation 12:4). Dr. Lutzer
   suggests that the number of fallen angels might include
   hundreds of millions. What does that tell us about the
   extent and power of the enemy and his forces? Do you
   ever find yourself underestimating the magnitude of the
   war that is raging for our souls?

2. Christ taught us that Satan was "a murderer from the beginning" and "is a liar and the father of lies" (John 8:44). It was Satan who lied to Adam and Eve and engineered their spiritual deaths. In Genesis 4:1–10, we learn that Cain murdered Abel and lied about it. How was the father of lies at work with the religious leaders of Jesus' day? What parallels can we see with the way the religious leaders dealt with Jesus?

   Jesus did miracls

3. Satan has continued to use his strategies of lies throughout history. In 2 Samuel 11, we read that David the adulterer became a liar, a schemer, and then a murderer. What satanic lies did David buy into? What do we know of some of the unintended consequences of his sins?

   Lust after Bathsheba

4. Why are we so often lured by temptation? What can we assume Satan and his minions know about each of us? Certainly, harboring unconfessed sin in our lives is an open invitation to Satan's strategies. What approaches can we take to deny the devil a foothold in our lives?

5. As Dr. Lutzer points out, Satan's strategy is to not only give people what they want, but to also make sure they get eventually what he wants them to have. How might we find ourselves getting caught in this trap? What can we do to defend ourselves against this deception?

6. Satan wants our circumstances to appear ordinary and his traps unsuspicious. Read the apostle Paul's warning in 2 Corinthians 11:3–4. (See also 10:10–11.) What are some of the devices Satan uses to attack believers?

7. Read Titus 1:1–2; 2 Timothy 1:9; Hebrews 13:20; and John 17:23–24. As believers, what do these verses tell us about the scope of our salvation?

8. Adam and Eve were deceived by an animal even though they possessed a God-given dominion over the world around them. What could they have done with the serpent by acting on their God-given responsibility? (Read Genesis 1:26.) What consequences ensued from Adam's "dropping the scepter"?

9. Colossians 1:16 tells us that the focus of creation is Jesus Christ. What does this rich passage tell us about how encompassing God's plan is?

10. Hebrews 13:20 tells us that we are saved through the "blood of the eternal covenant." With whom was this agreement made?

PERSONAL REFLECTION

S truggle as we might with the mysteries of God's plan, we can simply rejoice in Paul's words, "Even as he chose us in him before the foundation of the world, that we should be holy and blameless before him" (Ephesians 1:4). There is little use trying to explain this text by resorting to fanciful ideas about how for God eternity past is actually now. We should simply take delight in the fact that He did the choosing, and that He did it before the world was created.

When Adam and Eve sinned, God's plans were not thwarted nor needed adjustments to allow for their sin. God's plan encompasses everything. Colossians 1:16 tells us that everything exists *in* Him, *for* Him, and *through* Him. Jesus Christ planned and produced creation, and He did it for His own pleasure. We can be confident that all things are under His command. If everything in creation exists for Him, then nothing can be evil of itself, except for Satan and fallen angels, and even those God uses to accomplish His will.

There is no question that we are in a society where countless people have not only absorbed Satan's lies but live by them. As Christians in a fallen world, we are to be salt (Matthew 5:13) and light (Matthew 5:14–16) to those with whom we come in contact. According to 2 Corinthians 5:19–21, Paul calls us "ambassadors for Christ" with the message of the gospel. Let us show Christ to the world not only by how we conduct our lives, but may we also be ready to give an answer for the faith that is within us.

ENGAGING THE TOPIC answers:

1. lie   2. God, devil   3. good, detriment   4. Death
5. spiritually, eternally   6. harmless   7. occult

God's Devil, Chapter 4:

THE SERPENT'S NEW RELIGION

A Summary from the Book

For a moment, let's try to enter into the mind of Satan. What if you had a hateful passion to deceive everyone who inhabits the planet Earth? What if you had the ability to inject thoughts into the minds of some people that they think are their own? You are consumed with a desire to be worshiped. But you can't reveal your own evil nature to the human race and expect to be accepted.

So you set up a rival religion that makes sense to man, but you control it backstage. Your goal is to convince humans that they are experiencing God, when in fact they are actually in contact with you. Being worshiped under a disguise is better than not being worshiped at all. And so it was that in the garden of Eden the roots of occult religion began. Satan was not trying to disprove the existence of God in his temptation of Adam and Eve. He was competing with God for the allegiance of men.

Occultism has many forms, but it usually has five major premises. Whether the religions of the East or the flowering of contemporary New Age thought, all are fruits that have blossomed from the seeds planted in Eden. On that fateful day, Satan revealed the lies by which he would attempt to deceive the world. You will recognize them easily: the lies of reincarnation, esotericism, pantheism, relativism, and hedonism.

ENGAGING THE TOPIC

Complete the statements below after reading the book and the above summary. Then, during your class or small-group meeting, watch the DVD, Session 4.

1. Reincarnation is based on the cruel doctrine of
   Karma

2. Karma teaches that there is no _Injustice_ in the world.

3. Satan's most dazzling deception: a _counterfeit_ religious experience.

4. In reality, esotericism involves an encounter with a
   a Spiritual Being.

5. One implication if pantheism is that man is his own
   Saviour

6. The lie of relativism says that since man is his own
   __God__ , he is free to write his own __rules__

7. Only God can __restore__ the beauty of a marred creation.

QUESTIONS FOR DISCUSSION

1. Read carefully the words of God's message to Adam in Genesis 2:16–17 regarding the tree of the knowledge of good and evil. Now read Genesis 3:1–4. Compare the accounts. What subtle differences do you notice between God's words and the words the serpent chose?

2. Read Genesis 3:4, comparing it with Genesis 2:17. What was the serpent's lie? Discuss the doctrine of karma, which is at the root of the lie of *reincarnation*. How does this lie play out in the souls of men and women?

3. In Genesis 3:5, Satan's promise to Eve was "your eyes will be opened." Describe the philosophy of *esotericism*. What is Satan' strategy with this lie?

4. What is the lie of *pantheism*? What are its implications? Read the apostle Paul's warning about the coming Antichrist in 2 Thessalonians 2:11.

5. In Genesis 3:5, Satan espouses the lie of relativism by telling Adam and Eve, "You will be like God, knowing good and evil." What was Satan promising them with this lie? What problems would they encounter believing and trying to live this lie?

6. What examples of relativism do we see in our culture? How strongly do you believe our society today is being influenced by this lie?

7. In Satan's own words, "I will ascend above the heights of the clouds; I will make myself like the Most High" (Isaiah 14:14). In thinking that he could be like God, Satan blatantly rebelled against the Almighty. Because there was no one to tempt Lucifer, from where did his temptation to rebel come?

8. Read Genesis 3:6. What motivated Eve to disobey God? What was her error?

9. Although the word *hedonism* is often associated with a commitment to sexual pleasure, it has a broader application in our society. What is at the core of this doctrine?

10. Read Genesis 3:15. What three key truths can we determine from this passage? What did Satan fail to foresee?

PERSONAL REFLECTION

We must be careful students of God's Word, and be obedient to what it teaches. The apostle Paul wrote, "All Scripture is breathed out by God and profitable for teaching, for reproof, for correction, and for training in righteousness" (2 Timothy 3:16). In Genesis 3:1–5, notice that Satan questioned God's Word, denied God's warning to Adam (2:17), and substituted a lie for God's truth. It was a complete package of deception. Today, people continue to believe Satan's lies. As believers, we need to be on guard, for Satan still uses these same tactics to drive us to disobey God.

In Genesis 3:5, Satan's lie of relativism, "you will be like God, knowing good and evil," is his master lie. Read Isaiah

14:12–14 and Roman 1:21–25. Satan's high ambitions caused him to rebel against God. Obviously, Satan believed his own lie. We must be aware that he will perpetrate that lie to all who will believe it and join in his rebellion against God. Expect that the enemy will try repeatedly to get us to buy into his lie that we can be our own god. We prepare ourselves and protect ourselves by putting on the whole armor of God (Ephesians 6:10–18). Specifically, it is the "belt of truth" that protects us from the lies of the enemy that we have encountered in this chapter. As believers, our standard of truth is the Word of God.

Genesis 3:16 teaches us an important lesson regarding spiritual warfare. We see that rebelling against God is neither fun nor productive. For after Adam and Eve sinned, the tree they ate from was no longer alluring. They found the results of their sin to be chaotic and destructive. The consequences of their fall are all round us today. In Romans 5:12–21, we find the good news that we can rejoice that, through sacrifice of Christ on the cross, we can be saved from the punishment of our sin. Because of Adam we die; because of Christ we have eternal life.

ENGAGING THE TOPIC answers:

1. karma 2. injustice 3. counterfeit 4. Spiritual being
5. savior 6. God, rules 7. restore

God's Devil, Chapter 5:

THE SERPENT STRIKES BACK

A Summary from the Book

The contractor in our opening illustration experienced the law of unintended consequences firsthand. He thought he could control the fallout of his dishonesty but discovered that unforeseen events had been built into the temptation. One single act had repercussions he could not have anticipated. The can of soda was not what it appeared to be.

If not innocently, at least naively, Adam and Eve disobeyed God without realizing that they were setting in motion a moral and spiritual earthquake that would reverberate throughout the universe. They, like Lucifer before them, had no idea of the moral and spiritual aftershocks their single act of disobedience might generate. They must have been surprised that one small evil produced an endless chain of larger ones.

We have learned already the angels were created individually and fell individually; they have no mother or father. But in the case of man, the entire race was to descend from Adam and Eve; thus, when they sinned, they took all of their descendants with them. From that point on, every human being would be tainted with the sin virus.

The serpent strikes wherever he can with his deadly poison. Though he knows his doom is sure, he fights as if he has a chance. Just the thought of victory must satisfy him. He must be content with the knowledge that he would nip the heel of the woman's offspring. If he celebrates, it is always too soon.

Time and again God allowed Satan to make what might appear to be a fatal blow against the plan of God only to discover that he has been outwitted. No matter how close the contest seems to be,

God always has the last move on the chessboard.

The serpent will make a series of strikes against God and His people. He will try to divide the family; he will try to corrupt society; and he will try to kill the offspring seed. But God holds the trump card.

ENGAGING THE TOPIC

Complete the statements below after reading the book and the above summary. Then, during your class or small-group meeting, watch the DVD, Session 5.

1. The will of God is something all of us would choose if we had all the _____.

2. The discord within the first family mirrored the _____ of the whole human race.

3. Satan's delusions feed on the deception of _____
   _____.

4. Satan's primary strategy is directed toward _____
   _____.

5. In the Old Testament Satan's enemy was Israel, in our
   age it is the _____.

6. Believers stand with Christ in His _____.

QUESTIONS FOR DISCUSSION

1. In Dr. Lutzer's opening illustration, the contractor
   experienced the law of unintended consequences. A
   single act of sin or disobedience can bring unforeseen
   consequences. How is Satan so successful in getting his
   victims to take their temptations and sin so lightly?

2. Since Satan knows his doom is certain, what drives him
   to continue his mission?

3. Why does Satan's strategy include attacking the family? What does he hope to accomplish?

4. Read Jude 10–11. What is the "way of Cain"? What lesson does it teach us?

5. What does Genesis 6:1–2 describe? What do we understand the phrase "sons of God" to mean? Read God's response in Genesis 6:5–8. How did he defeat Satan once again?

6. What important lesson do we draw from Christ's words in Matthew 24:37–39?

7. Why is Satan's primary strategy directed toward God's people? Who were his targets in the Old and New Testaments? Who will be his target in the last days? (See Revelation 12.)

8. Today, through doctrinal confusion and moral degradation, Satan continues his relentless attack on God's people. What does he hope to accomplish with these tactics?

9. Why are Satan's victories in his conflict with God only illusionary? Why does allow Satan to win certain battles?

10. Christ invites us to participate in His victory over Satan. What encouragement did Elisha give his servant in 2 Kings 6:16–17? What encouragement can we take away from this account?

PERSONAL REFLECTION

Read 1 John 3:9–12. Cain had opened his life to an unseen enemy. He chose to nurture his jealousy rather than confess it and find mercy. John tells us that "we should not be like Cain, who was of the evil one" (1 John 3:12). No one born of God should make a practice of sinning. With the believer, deliberate sin grieves the Holy Spirit (Ephesians 4:30). Because the children of God have a new nature, the way they live should reveal that new nature. For the children of God, the Word of God (1 Peter 1:23) and the Spirit of God (John 3:6) are spiritual parents. The Spirit of God uses the Word of God to convict us of sin and to reveal the Savior to us.

Our families are strategic units. God designed the family to propagate the faith from one generation to another. Fathers are to teach their children about God, and their children are to teach their children. The serpent's poison spills beyond our homes into our churches, schools, and offices. Let us place Christ at the center of our homes and raise our families by establishing God's Word as the standard.

ENGAGING THE TOPIC answers:

1. facts   2. division   3. a possible victory   4. God's people
5. church   6. triumph

God's Devil, Chapter 6:

THE SERPENT IS CRUSHED

A Summary from the Book

There was a scuffle as the serpent thrashed about, his fangs upright, hissing at his opponent. As the loathsome beast lay gasping, it attempted to strike but could only nip the heel of the foot that stepped on its head. When the frenzy was over, the head of the serpent lay crushed, pounded in the hard dirt, its body throbbing in pain. While drops of its poison lay spent on the ground, the victor returned to heaven in triumph.

At last, Christ was here. Centuries earlier God had said to the serpent, "I will put enmity between you and the woman, and between your offspring and her offspring; he shall bruise your head, and you shall bruise his heel" (Genesis 3:15). God had made good on His word.

When Christ was born in Bethlehem, Satan's first strategy was to kill Him. Wicked King Herod tried to carry out the diabolical deed. But Joseph and Mary took the baby to Egypt, and the plan was foiled.

If Satan could not kill Christ, he would seek to corrupt Him with temptations. Once Satan saw Christ was headed to Jerusalem, he stopped trying to prevent the cross and chose to be a player in the drama. If Christ was going to the cross, the serpent wanted the satisfaction of knowing that he had a part in it.

The cross, incredibly enough, is about us. Take note that the conflict between God and Satan is always waged over us; we are the trophies. If we are believers in Christ, Satan cannot have our souls, but he will try to destroy our fellowship with God. Satan will do all he can to dispute God's plans and judgment. But God will always win the battle for those who are His.

Just how He won the battle for us is the subject of this chapter.

ENGAGING THE TOPIC

Complete the statements below after reading the book and the above summary. Then, during your class or small-group meeting, watch the DVD, Session 6.

1. If _____ belonged to Satan, _____ belonged to God.

2. We are sinners, both by _____ and by _____.

3. Christ reconciled sinners to God by _____ .

4. Although the forces who war against us have had their _____ removed, they continue to fight.

5. We were declared righteous by _____ High Priest, _____ offering, _____ act of justification.

6. Satan can only _____ ; he cannot make _____ .

QUESTIONS FOR DISCUSSION

1. For what three reasons do we know that the cross was a time of satanic conflict? Read John 13:27; Luke 22:52–53; John 12:31–32.

2. What does it mean to say that the cross crushed the head of the serpent? And how were we included in Christ's victory over the serpent?

3. Can Christ reconcile us to Himself and still retain His integrity? How do we have the right to God forever despite the fact that we are members of a race that sided with Satan?

4. Read Zechariah 3:1–7. In this "courtroom" scene, Joshua the high priest is standing before God with Satan standing at Joshua's right hand, accusing him. How does this scene play out? What is God's verdict? On what basis did God deliver His verdict? If you were the one standing before God instead of Joshua, would God's verdict be different?

5. Read Ezekiel 18:4 and Romans 6:23. What do these verses convey? In Romans 3:19, Paul, acting as an attorney, summarizes the case. What is his conclusion? What is our predicament?

6. Read Colossians 2:13–15. What do we learn from this passage? (See also 1 Peter 2:24.)

7. Satan's accusations against us follows one of two directions. What are those directions? What if his strategy fails?

8. Christ's last words from the cross were, "It is finished." What does that remarkable statement convey? What Old Testament prophecies can you identify were fulfilled by this sacrificial event? (See Hebrews 10:1–18.)

9. Hebrews 2:5–13 teaches that that believers are exalted above the angels. (The Old Testament quotation here in Hebrews is from Psalm 8:4–6.) What higher privileges has man been given? (See also Ephesians 3:10.)

10. Today, God allows Satan to roam until his final judgment. Why has God postponed his sentence to the lake of fire and allowed Satan his current freedom?

PERSONAL REFLECTION

Second Corinthians 5:21 tells us that "for our sake he made him to be sin who knew no sin, so that in him we might become the righteousness of God." We can scarcely comprehend what the weight of all sin—past, present, and future—felt to Him.

We must never lose sight of the truth that He made our condemnation His. He accepted it, exhausted it, and annihilated it on His cross. By God's grace, we receive reconciliation when we humble ourselves to be forgiven and restored at this infinite cost.

Christ's death opened heaven to those who are His children. There is now a direct route to heaven by the One who Himself has entered. Therefore, for the believer, death is no longer an enemy but a friend that takes us to heaven. Second Corinthians 5:8 Paul tells the Corinthians, "We would rather be away from the body and at home with the Lord." Because of this assurance, we can have confidence in this life during trials and suffering, and have no fear of death. Christ has taken the "sting" out of death. Let us draw courage from the knowledge that Christ's resurrection proved He was stronger than the grave.

John 19:30 gives us Christ's last words on the cross: "It is finished." The original Greek text from which our English versions are translated uses one Greek word: *tetelesti*. It was a word used in everyday life in Jesus' day. His listeners knew exactly what it meant. The Greek language tense used for this word means, "It is finished, it stands finished, and will always be finished!" Christ's death on the cross was an eternal sacrifice and so are its results! At the cross, Satan was defeated forever. We can thank God daily that Christ's work on the cross is done.

ENGAGING THE TOPIC answers:

1. time, eternity 2. nature, choice 3. by the cross
4. authority 5. one, one, one 6. kill, alive

God's Devil, Chapter 7:

THE SERPENT, GOD'S SERVANT

A Summary from the Book

How much power do you think Satan has? The question can be answered accurately: the devil has exactly as much power as God lets him have, and not a mite more!

Sometimes I think the devil enjoys much of the renewed attention he has received in the last thirty or so years! My point is simply that in much of the literature his ability to wield power is grossly overestimated. Some teachers, having finally understood that we all are affected by Satan or one of his emissaries, have made demonic exorcism to be the primary means of breaking stubborn habits or dealing with a painful past.

At best, Satan is found to be the cause of virtually every

problem; at worst, he has been thought to be well nigh all-powerful. Rather than inspiring faith, such counseling has led to helpless pessimism. Oh, yes, God will win in the end, but in this world, we are told, Satan has free rein to do whatever he wishes. Though most agree at the end of the day God will win, some people live and talk as if it will be a close finish. Well, it won't be!

The devil is just as much God's servant in his rebellion as he was God's servant in the days of his sweet obedience. Even today, he cannot act without God's express permission; he cannot tempt, coerce, demonize, nor make so much as a single plan without consent and approval of God. We can't quote Martin Luther too often: The devil is God's devil.

ENGAGING THE TOPIC

Complete the statements below after reading the book and the above summary. Then, during your class or small-group meeting, watch the DVD, Session 7.

1. Satan is not free to simply wreak havoc on people at
   _____.

2. Satan has different roles to play, depending on God's
   _____ and _____.

3. God and the devil are both involved in our _____
   and _____.

4. God uses Satan to _____ the unconverted.

5. God uses Satan to _____ the obedient.

6. Satan is given to us that we might _____ against him.

7. Only God has _____ authority over Satan.

QUESTIONS FOR DISCUSSION

1. For what reason has God kept Satan in the world and not sent him directly into the lake of fire?

2. Read 2 Corinthians 4:4 and Mark 4:15. What do these passages teach us about Satan's work of blinding the minds of unbelieving people? For what purpose does God allow Satan the power to judge the unconverted?

3. God's people have a role in helping people "see the light." Read Romans 1:16 and John 6:35. What assurances do we have from Scripture that, with the help of the Holy Spirit, that those given to Christ by the Father would come to Him and be received? (See also John 10:28–29; 17:6; Ephesians 1:4.)

4. Read Job 1–2 as background. For what reasons did God allow Satan to afflict Job? What was Job's response to all that Satan dealt him? What do we learn from Job's story that we might apply to our lives?

5. Read Exodus 20:5–6. To what extent are the iniquities of the father "visited upon the children"? Discuss Dr. Lutzer's observations on this question.

6. With regard to God's disciplining the disobedient, what principle do we learn from Deuteronomy 28:47–48? How did this principle play out with King Saul in 1 Samuel 18? See also New Testament examples in 1 Corinthians 5:6 and 1 Timothy 1:20.

7. Read the account of the apostle Paul's "thorn ... in the flesh" in 2 Corinthians 12:7. What was Paul's response in verses 9–10? How was he able to accept his "thorn ... in the flesh"? Why is it helpful for us to thank God for such afflictions?

8. God and Satan have different purposes for our demonic conflicts. We must distinguish between what God wants and what Satan wants. What does God seek with our testing? What does Satan want to accomplish? What steps can we take to help turn our trials into victories?

9. When experiencing demonic conflict, we must also distinguish between God's authority and our authority. Who holds absolute authority over Satan? Ephesians 2:6 tells us that we are "seated us with him in the heavenly places in Christ Jesus." How should we properly defer what authority we are given to God's absolute authority?

10. Read Revelation 2:10, which summarizes the thrust of this chapter. Dr. Lutzer presents three important points culled from this verse. What truths do we learn from each?

PERSONAL REFLECTION

Christians who can give thanks for their demonic afflictions are usually the first to experience the freedom of Christ in their lives. As we understand that our trials are ultimately from God and not the enemy, we can start to see the larger purpose. We must remember that God often balances our blessing with our trials to help us grow spiritually.

We can give thanks for the way God uses our struggles and temptations to accomplish His purposes in our lives.

Dr. Lutzer states that "only in the flames of temptation and trial are we purified." We must often remind ourselves that we are a work in progress. As children of God, we never need faint in times of suffering and trial because we know that God is at work on our behalf. According to Romans 8:29, we are being "conformed to the image of his Son." Everything God does in our life is to increase our joy, if not in this life, then in the life to come. Ultimately, He will make us like Jesus Christ!

Sometimes Satan's role is to be the agent of God's discipline. We recall David's words before he repented, "For day and night your hand was heavy upon me; my strength was dried up as by the heat of summer" (Psalm 32:4). Those were the words of a man who knew the torments of God's discipline. Read 1 Samuel 30:1–8, which describes David's return to Ziklag. With the city burned to the ground and the women and children taken captive, David found himself at the end of his rope. In his distress, "David strengthened himself in the Lord his God" (v. 6). He restored his fellowship with God and realigned with God's will. Sometimes God will allow circumstances and attacks from the enemy to bring us back into fellowship with Him.

ENGAGING THE TOPIC answers:

1. will   2. counsel, purposes   3. temptations, struggles
4. judge   5. refine   6. fight   7. unlimited

PLEASE NOTE: This DVD session 8 includes both chapters 8 and 9 of *God's Devil*.

God's Devil, Chapter 8:	*God's Devil*, Chapter 9:
WHAT THE SERPENT WANTS FROM YOU	CLOSING THE DOOR WHEN THE SERPENT KNOCKS

A Summary from the Book

Chapter 8: "What the Serpent Wants from You"

We're in a war. The struggle keeps raging even after we have walked with God for years. Part of it is the struggle between flesh and spirit; part of it is Satan who harasses with his ideas and rationalizations and by magnifying our desires.

Sins we thought were gone keep cropping up unexpectedly.

As one man said, "The devil is now coming to collect for the sins I committed in my youth."

What does the devil want from me and you? In short, he wants us to sin that our souls will be separated from God. He wants us to reject God's authority, just as he did, so that we might share his fate. We are the targets of his fury and relentless attacks. All this is to promote his consuming desire: recognition and worship. He wants us to be like him.

If we are believers, Satan knows he cannot keep us from God's love and that our souls are eternally secure, since we are God's children. The best he can do is break our fellowship with God; he wants us to be contaminated with sin so that God is obscured. If he cannot keep us from heaven, at least he can keep us from usefulness on earth.

Satan's chief method is to make sin look good to us. He does not want us to fear disobedience, but to develop confidence in our ability to control it and its consequences. Sins of all shapes and sizes come wrapped in the most attractive packages. He does not explain the law of unintended consequences.

Let us take a walk in the Judean desert and relive the conflict between the serpent and Christ. Here we see a classic battle, and we can learn from the outcome.

ENGAGING THE TOPIC

Complete the statements below after reading the book and the above summary. Then, during your class or small-group meeting, watch the DVD, Session 8.

1. In Christ's wilderness testing, He proved that His devotion to God was greater than His _____.

2. God wanted to prove that Christ would _____ in every arena of temptation where Adam _____.

3. _____ is the devil's most persistent weapon.

4. God is _____ when we believe the truth of His Word is stronger than the error of Satan's lies.

QUESTIONS FOR DISCUSSION

1. Read Hebrews 4:15 and 1 John 2:16. How do we identify with Christ's experience of temptation?

2. Read Matthew 4:3–4. (See also Deuteronomy 8:3.) What was Satan's first temptation attempt? How did Christ respond? What does it teach us? (See also John 4:32–34.)

3. Read Matthew 4:6. (See also Deuteronomy 6:16.) What was Satan's second temptation attempt? Why was it trickier than the first temptation? Describe Christ's response. What do we learn from this temptation?

4. Read Matthew 4:8–11. (See also Deuteronomy 6:13.) What was Satan tempting Christ to do? How did Christ respond to this third attempt? What do we learn from this temptation?

5. Why is *despair* a powerful weapon of Satan? How can it negatively impact one's faith?

6. The book of James tells us that we are tempted when we are carried away and enticed by our own lusts. Drawing from the progression presented in James 1:15, how would you describe the impact and severity of uncontrolled lust? As believers, how must we guard ourselves from falling prey to Satan's deceptive traps?

PERSONAL REFLECTION

When Satan tempted Jesus in the desert to turn away from God's will and perform a miracle before its time, Jesus refused. Satan will also tempt us to abandon God's will as it is revealed in the Scriptures. Our challenge is to have faith to believe God's way is best, even when it doesn't appear to be so on the surface. Let us not assume that we always know what is best. In John 4:34, Jesus taught his disciples, "My food is to do the will of him who sent me and to complete his work." Anchoring ourselves in the Word of God and meditating on its truths strengthens us against Satan's attempts to turn us away from God's will for us.

In our walk with God, there will be times when our faith will be challenged. Dr. Lutzer points out that closed doors are given to us that our faith and persistence might be tested. God can accomplish His purposes through both open and closed doors. We must never forget that He has ultimate authority and holds the key to our sufferings, our successes, and our struggles with the devil. When the enemy tempts us with his lies, we must claim James 4:7, "Submit yourselves therefore to God. Resist the devil, and he will flee from you."

In Genesis 22, when God asked Abraham to sacrifice his son, Isaac, Abraham faced an enormous test. He was victorious because he trusted God. Abraham was transformed by temptation because he endured it successfully. As a result, he blessed where his testing took place, naming it "Jehovah-jireh," which means "God will provide." God uses our testing for His purposes.

James 1:13–14 tells us, "Let no one say when he is tempted, 'I am being tempted by God,' for God cannot be tempted with evil, and he himself tempts no one. But each person is tempted when he is lured and enticed by his own desire." God does not tempt us or lure to do evil, but He does allow us to be tested to give us an opportunity to show how much we love Him.

When facing temptation that might seem too much to overcome, take time to read and claim the promise of 1 Corinthians 10:13: "No temptation has overtaken you that is not common to man. God is faithful, and he will not let you be tempted beyond your ability, but with the temptation he will also provide the way of escape, that you may be able to endure it." God knows how much we can endure. At times, the way of escape may simply be to flee (see v. 14; 6:18).

ENGAGING THE TOPIC answers (Chapter 8):

1. human desires   2. win, failed   3. Despair   4. glorified

A Summary from the Book

PLEASE NOTE: This chapter 9 study is a continuation of DVD, Session 8.

Chapter 9: "Closing the Door When the Serpent Knocks"

Satan has a master plan to deceive the nations of the world. He hopes to redefine our definition of God so we are willing to switch our allegiances. The evil one wants us to end up worshiping him rather than the living and true God.

But he also has a personal plan for your life. He has a niche for you in his overall scheme. He believes he can get us to follow him, at least for a part of the journey. He plants seeds he hopes will germinate years later. He stays out of view, waiting for that special moment. He knows that he himself is abhorrent to us, so he comes in different disguises, using different names and different interests.

Of special interest is our secret life, those attitudes and behaviors we keep from others. Evil spirits are probably not able to read the minds of believers, but they observe our actions. This provides them with their most fruitful areas of temptation.

I believe Satan has already made meticulous plans for our downfall. All that is left for us to do is to step into the trap that has been carefully laid. Of course, we don't know where the trap is, nor can we see it, but it is there nevertheless.

We must remember three principles that drive Satan: (1) he is angry at God; (2) his method is to make sin look good to us; and (3) he works through the sins of the flesh. What does he want from us? Control. He wants the privilege of controlling our lives.

There are some doors the devil hopes we will open, if only just a crack. These are the doors that give him an occasion to develop a stronghold, that is, a pattern of sinful behavior that enables him to exert influence on us. Some of the most obvious doors are: rebellion/self-will, anger, hatred/murder, guilt, false religions, fear, sexual immorality, and perversions.

We will discuss how we can close those doors and keep them closed.

ENGAGING THE TOPIC

Complete the statements below after reading the book and the above summary. Then, during your class or small-group meeting, watch the DVD, Session 8.

1. Satan's chief method is to make sin look _____ to us.

2. Satan will never remind us of the law of _____ consequences.

3. Satan works through the sins of the _____.

4. _____ is at the root of all our sins.

QUESTIONS FOR DISCUSSION

1. Chapter 8 focused on what Satan wants from us. In contrast, Dr. Lutzer also explains what God wants. Discuss the points he presents.

2. Dr. Lutzer identifies three principles that drive Satan as he seeks to entrap us: his anger toward God, making sin look good to us, and focusing on the sins of the flesh—the sins we already struggle with. What does he do to employ those principles and make them effective?

3. Satan uses three successive stages, or levels, of control to subvert us: *temptation, obsession,* and *possession.* Discuss the dynamics involved with each of those stages. How does one stage lead to the next?

4. Can Christians be possessed by demons? What are some of the difficulties for clearly answering this question?

5. Dr. Lutzer identifies "seven doors" to our fallen nature that should remain closed to Satan. What are these doors, and what consequences can they bring if left opened for Satan to do his work?

6. Read the challenges given to us in 1 Peter 5:8–9, James 4:7, and Ephesians 6:11. Discuss the meaning of the word *resist*. What does it involve for the believer?

We must always be on guard for attacks from the enemy. First Peter 5:8–9 tells us, "Be sober-minded; be watchful. Your adversary the devil prowls around like a roaring lion, seeking someone to devour. Resist him, firm in your faith, knowing that the same kinds of suffering are being experienced by your brotherhood throughout the world." Never underestimate the evil one. He is powerful and we must learn to respect that power. We can resist his attacks if we put on the full armor of God and trust the Holy Spirit to strengthen us (Ephesians 6:10–20).

Satan can tempt us by giving us ideas. Whether or not we act on them is our choice. As a defense, we must constantly guard our thoughts and not let down our guard. We must resolve to not give Satan a beachhead from which to operate. We may claim several verses of Scripture to help us protect our thought life.

- "Do not be conformed to this world, but be transformed by the renewal of your mind, that by testing you may discern what is the will of God, what is good and acceptable and perfect" (Romans 12:2).

- "And the peace of God, which surpasses all understanding, will guard your hearts and your minds in Christ Jesus" (Philippians 4:7).

- "You keep him in perfect peace whose mind is stayed on you, because he trusts in you" (Isaiah 26:3).

Those passages do not teach that we will not face trials on the outside, but they promise a quiet confidence within during our trials.

As we submit to the power of God's Word, the devil will flee. We must quote Scripture often, even when the resistance heightens. We must stay with truth no matter how many grenades are "lobbed" in our direction from the enemy. There are times when the temptations are so overwhelming that we must wholeheartedly find our refuge in God. Such victories are the most precious to Him.

ENGAGING THE TOPIC answers (Chapter 9):

1. good   2. unintended   3. flesh   4. Self-will

God's Devil, Chapter 10:

NEUTRALIZING THE SERPENT'S POISON

A Summary from the Book

Would you be offended if I were to say that we have some of the same characteristics as the devil? We should not be surprised if we do, for a little drop of his rebellion has fallen on every human heart. We may no longer belong to the devil, but we sometimes act like him.

Of course, as believers we also have the characteristics of Christ. God's express purpose in saving us is to make us more like Himself; we are to be His sons and daughters. We are involved in a conflict: We are poised between God and the devil, each desiring our loyalty, each wishing to turn us into his likeness.

Christians can, at times, have the characteristics of Satan,

71

for we still struggle in our fallenness. We can be bitter, rebellious, and malicious. In fact, there are more parallels than we care to admit.

Satan wants us to sin so we will be like him; God wants us to renounce evil and be filled with the Holy Spirit so that we will be like His Son. The more intense the temptation, the greater the triumph. As Christians we have changed kingdoms and must now change our loyalties. But the battle within and without is intense. Satan tempts us with evil, but at the end of the day it is we who do what we want to do.

Our task is to identify the fruit of rebellion and give Satan "no place." If we are successful in our struggle against temptation, God is glorified. Though we abhor the devil, we find ourselves comfortable with his attitudes and behaviors. James speaks of the tongue as being evil and full of "deadly poison" (James 3:8–9). That deadly poison has its source in the serpent.

I have chosen to discuss the following parallels between us and Satan because they remind us how easy we can be like our archenemy: verbal slander, a refusal to confess Christ, uncleanness, the desire for control, the love of praise, and deceit.

ENGAGING THE TOPIC

Complete the statements below after reading the book and the above summary. Then, during your class or small-group meeting, watch the DVD, Session 9.

1. The more _____ the temptation, the _____ the triumph.

2. _____ keeps me from letting God be the supreme ruler of my life.

3. God's express purpose in saving us is to make us more like _____.

4. God calls us to represent Him, not just by our _____ , but by our _____.

5. If you believe a lie, it becomes the _____ for you.

6. As we received _____ by faith, so we _____ by faith.

QUESTIONS FOR DISCUSSION

1. Read Galatians 5:19–21. These sins of the flesh cover a wide range of behavior. To God, is any one of the sins in this list less acceptable than the others? What is at the root of these sins?

2. We struggle against an invisible enemy. If we were able to view Satan in the midst of our temptations to sin, would that change how attractive a sin might appear to us? However, we are not alone with such struggles. We know that God sees and is willing to help us with our temptations. How may we be encouraged by that?

3. In 1 Timothy 3:11, Paul, in setting forth the qualifications for the wives of deacons, wrote about avoiding verbal slander. Describe the nature of slander. In what ways is slander damaging to others? (See also James 3:8–9.)

4. Read 1 Corinthians 12:3. What is this passage teaching us?

5. Mark 5:2 gives an account of a man having "an unclean spirit." Describe what it means to have "an unclean spirit." How do unclean spirits impact us? Discuss examples of unclean spirits we need to avoid in our lives. As believers, what is our remedy for an unclean spirit? (See also 2 Peter 2:10.)

6. Why is the desire for control a sin of the flesh? What is at the root of this sin? Discuss examples of control that are not honoring to God.

7. Why is Satan's love of praise a sin? What are some ways we fall prey to this same sin?

8. Why is deceit tricky? Read Jeremiah 17:9. How do we allow ourselves to become deceived?

9. What is the cure for self-will that leads to the sins of the flesh? What does "putting an ax to the root of tree" require from us?

10. Dr. Lutzer presents four truths that guide us as we attempt to neutralize the serpent's poison in our lives. Follow the author's discussion of each of these truths, engaging the accompanying Scriptures passages:

- We must believe Christ has made our death to self-rule possible (Romans 6:6, 12)
- We must be repentant, that is, come to the end of our rationalizations and excuses
- We must receive the filling of the Holy Spirit (Galatians 5:16, 22–23)
- The key is faith

PERSONAL REFLECTION

One of Satan's activities is to tempt us so we might plant seeds of sin in our lives that he hopes will germinate and grow into bigger sins, especially if we should cultivate them. If not dealt with, such sins could surface even years later. In his book *The Strategy of Satan* (Tyndale House, 1979), Warren Wiersbe has a chapter titled, "Don't Give Satan a Beachhead." The point is that known or cultivated sin in our lives can provide Satan a beachhead from which he can operate in our lives. The sins of the flesh, the focus of this chapter, are those kinds of sins. If you are struggling with harbored sin in your life, ask God to help you "put to death the deeds of the body" (Romans 8:13; Romans 6:6, 12). Anchor yourself in His Word, trusting Him for the victory.

Jeremiah 17:9–10 tells us that our hearts are "sick." We may think we know our own hearts, but we cannot. The human heart is in a desperate spiritual state. Only God can search our hearts and know what is there. And we might be surprised what He finds. Ask God, the Great Physician, to search and probe the hidden depths of your heart. Be willing to obey God's Word regarding what God lays on your heart. Allowing the Holy Spirit to minister to your heart, ask God to exercise His healing power.

In Galatians 5:19–21, the list of sins the devil can tempt us with is formidable. Ephesians 4:27 tells to "give no opportunity to the devil." As we struggle against the sins of the flesh, we need to be aware that at the root of sin is self-will, the desire to resist God's sovereignty in our lives. We must constantly be on guard to control our thoughts desires or we may become vulnerable to attacks from the enemy. In your daily walk of faith, ask God to give you the strength to make the tough choices that will affect the source of sinful thoughts and behavior.

ENGAGING THE TOPIC answers:

1. intense, greater   2. Pride   3. Christ   4. lives, lips   5. truth
6. Christ, walk

DVD SESSION 10

PLEASE NOTE: This DVD session 10 includes both chapters 11 and 12 of *God's Devil*.

God's Devil, Chapter 11:	*God's Devil*, Chapter 12:
THE SERPENT IS CAST OUT OF HEAVEN	THE SERPENT IN ETERNAL HUMILIATION

A Summary from the Book

Chapter 11: "The Serpent Is Cast Out of Heaven"

God's judgment is often long in coming, but when it arrives, it is swift and sure. When God begins to wrap up human history as we know it, the demise of the serpent will happen in a series of stages. The lake of fire was inevitable from the moment Lucifer said, "I will make myself like the Most High" (Isaiah 14:14), but for centuries God has postponed the inevitable. When He no longer needs Satan for

His own purposes, the end shall come.

At the cross, the prince of this world was cast out (John 12:31). There Satan was judged and found to be guilty; his sentence of doom was held high for all to see. He was stripped of all authority and found to be deficient. As he writhed amid ashes of defeat and eventual doom, he was forced to concede that Christ was the victor. Satan took a blow to the head, whereas his retaliation was only a nip at Christ's heel. All things considered, Satan's was a pathetic show of strength.

Satan's final ruin comes in three stages. First, he is cast out of heaven (the subject of this chapter). Second, he is bound for a thousand years. Finally, he is cast into the lake of fire (the subject of the next chapter). He knows as well as we do that these judgments are on the horizon. When he thinks of the future, he is terrified.

The victory of the cross was now translated into a victory in heaven. The devil and his angels are thrown out and "lose their place in heaven." The serpent glances toward heaven for the last time and knows that for him the gates are now bolted shut.

Imagine his anger when he sees the gates of heaven close with the saints he had persecuted on earth now standing before the throne of God in the spotless beauty of Jesus! He sees them exalted above the angels, as brothers in Christ, though they had committed many of the same sins as he. He knows that they will be there forever; he knows where *he* will be forever. No wonder he is furious.

ENGAGING THE TOPIC

Complete the statements below after reading the book and the above summary. Then, during your class or small-group meeting, watch the DVD, Session 10.

1. The victory of the _____ is now translated to a victory in _____.

2. The beast, who is empowered by the dragon, corresponds to _____.

3. When Satan is thrown out of heaven he is angry because _____.

4. No matter how extensive Satan's end-time network, the power of the _____ still stands.

QUESTIONS FOR DISCUSSION

1. Does Satan have access to heaven today? Read Dr. Lutzer's discussion of this question. What suggests that Satan does have access?

2. Read Revelation 12. Describe the two great signs. What does the symbolism of this passage signify? What is special about the content of verse 5? Describe the second great sign in Revelation 12. (See also the supporting passage in Daniel 7:7–8)

3. Read Revelation 12:7–8, which describes the coming war in heaven. Why is it significant that Michael led God's angels to victory? Why does this victory correspond with Christ's victory at the cross?

4. Why is it reasonable to conclude that the war in heaven occurs during the middle of the tribulation period? (See Revelation 12:10–13; 11:2; 13:5; Daniel 7:25; 12:7.)

5. Read Revelation 13. Who are the members of Satan's
    unholy trinity? How does each member of that trinity
    correspond to the Holy Trinity?

6. Read Revelation 12:11. During the tribulation period,
    there will be a remnant of believers who will overcome
    the attack of Satan. What is the significance of the
    blood of Christ for the believer? How does the "blood
    of the Lamb" counter the attack of Satan?

PERSONAL REFLECTION

Our world system currently is under the control of the
enemy. The prince of this world and his army is un-
ceasingly at work. And his attacks are sometimes subtle.
Pressure to conform exists all around us, so we must always
be on guard. Whenever tempted to compromise, remember
Romans 12:2, "Do not be conformed to this world, but be
transformed by the renewal of your mind, that by testing
you may discern what is the will of God, what is good and
acceptable and perfect." Make it a point to begin each day

spending time with God's Word and in prayer, yielding your body, mind, and will to God.

Revelation 12:10–12 describes Satan as the accuser of God's people. (The name *devil* means "accuser.") He accuses us before the throne of God. But Satan's accusations fall short. "And they have conquered him by of the blood of the Lamb" (v. 11). We can be encouraged that because of the blood of the Lamb, Satan can no longer accuse those who have been acquitted by God, thanks to the sacrifice of Christ on the cross!

Although Satan is defeated and knows it, he remains persistent in persecuting and attacking God's people. As believers, we find that our walk of faith is a battleground. But God is able to shelter us and He is our refuge. He knows we face an enemy much stronger that we are. However, with the power of God and His Word, we overcome the enemy. In Ephesians 6:10–18, the apostle Paul exhorts us to put on the full armor of God to shield ourselves from the attacks and schemes of the enemy. Never let down your guard! Daily, make it a point to put on the full armor of God.

ENGAGING THE TOPIC answers (Chapter 11):

1. cross, heaven   2. Christ   3. his time is short   4. cross

A Summary from the Book

Chapter 12: "The Serpent in Eternal Humiliation"

We can only speculate what might have happened if Lucifer had been shown the lake of fire before he made his decision to rebel. If only he had believed that God always knows best, his tragic story might have read differently. But now, centuries of sadistic rebellion will never compensate for one hour in the lake of fire. And the fire will never be quenched.

In the Old Testament, God had repeatedly predicted a coming kingdom in which righteousness and justice would prevail. He spoke of a day when men will lay down their weapons and live together in tranquility and peace. This will be a kingdom in which Christ will rule.

Repeatedly, Satan has tried to usher in this kingdom under his own auspices. The Roman Empire, with its vast network of cruel armies, roads, and laws was the first clear attempt to unify the world and bring it under a central leadership. However, Satan discovered that he cannot control human beings at will; he cannot establish a kingdom on earth that is both organized and unified.

We have learned that the Bible teaches that Satan will make one more missive attempt to rule the world—and will finally succeed. By the time Antichrist appears, the world will be ready to attempt a dream that has been in the making since the days of Babylon when all the people chose to stay together, unified by a tower whose top would reach into heaven (Genesis 11:4). Given today's advance in technology and instant communication, a unified world will appear to be possible.

Satan will be thrown out of heaven in the middle of the tribulation period. It is his fury, knowing that his time is short, that will motivate him to take one last, daring gamble.

The saints of God will oppose him. The rulers of the world will move to protect their own selfish interests. This conflict, known as the battle of Armageddon, will be the worst in the history of the world. Jesus Christ Himself shall lead His people into victory.

In the end, the cosmic gamble failed. The destruction of the serpent in the lake of fire stands as a final witness to the fact that no creature who fights against the Creator will win.

ENGAGING THE TOPIC

Complete the statements below after reading the book and the above summary. Then, during your class or small-group meeting, watch the DVD, Session 12.

1. If the devil is God's _____ , then hell is God's _____.

2. The greatness of our sin is determined by the _____ of the being against whom it is committed.

3. Christ taught that hell was as _____ as heaven.

4. God judges with a full _____ of the _____.

QUESTIONS FOR DISCUSSION

1. In Revelation 19:11–21, John provides a detailed, graphic account of Christ's return and His ensuing victory. What are the results of this battle? Why is Satan spared from the lake of fire at this time?

2. What do we know about the "abyss" (Romans 10:7) (or, "bottomless pit") described in Revelation 20:1–3? The Greek word used in this text is *abussos*, which means literally "without bottom." (See also Revelation 9:1–2, 11; 11:7; 17:8.) Why does God bind Satan and his demons for one thousand years?

3. Discuss the three major views regarding the millennium: *premillennialism, postmillennialism,* and *amillennialism.* What is the key premise of each? For what key reasons does Dr. Lutzer give for holding to a premillennialism position?

4. Dr. Lutzer devotes several pages to the "lake of fire." Why did God create it? (See Matthew 25:41.)

5. Who are the occupants of the lake of fire? (See Revelation 20:11–15.)

6. Is everlasting punishment without any possibility of reform for the offense committed a just sentence? What is the basis of God's judgment?

PERSONAL REFLECTION

One of the reasons Satan exists is to be God's means of the purification of the obedient. Our war with the enemy teaches us about the nature of sin, the holiness of God, and our own helplessness apart from God's grace. Lucifer's fall gave our heavenly Father an opportunity to display limitless mercy toward us. He who rules all things by the counsel of His own will has triumphed, and we share His victory.

During this life, we may not fully comprehend the seriousness of sin. For those of us redeemed by the shed blood of Jesus, we ought to daily thank God that Jesus took the infinite guilt of our sins upon Himself. We will forever be thankful that an infinite Being came to pay an infinite price for our redemption. "To him who loves us and has freed us from our sins by his blood and made us a kingdom, priests to his God and Father, to him be glory and dominion forever and ever. Amen" (Revelation 1:5–6).

Reflect for a moment on the text of Romans 11:33–36. While we cannot fully understand God's purposes and plans, we can focus our minds and hearts on who He is. The more we learn about His attributes, perfections, and His ways, the more reason we will find to praise Him and worship Him!

We have learned in this study that God's wrath will eventually come. Only personal faith in Jesus Christ can shield us from that wrath. Only those who have faith in "the blood of the Lamb" can overcome the devil's fury and be spared of the wrath to come (Revelation 7:14; 12:11). If you are not a believer, acknowledge your helplessness apart from a saving knowledge of Jesus Christ.

ENGAGING THE TOPIC answers (Chapter 12):

1. devil, hell   2. greatness   3. eternal   4. knowledge, facts

MORE BOOKS BY ERWIN W. LUTZER

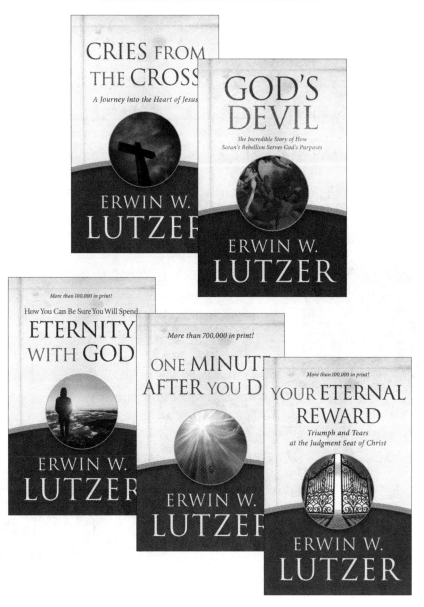

MOODY
Publishers™

From the Word to Life

ONE MINUTE
AFTER YOU DIE

More than 700,000 in print!

ONE MINUTE
AFTER YOU DIE

ERWIN
LUTZ

ONE MINUTE
AFTER YOU DIE

STUDY GUIDE

ERWIN
LUTZ

DVD

ONE MINUTE
AFTER YOU DIE

ERWIN W.
LUTZER

- Book
- Study Guide
- DVD

MOODY
Publishers™

From the Word to Life

DR. LUTZER'S AUTOBIOGRAPHY

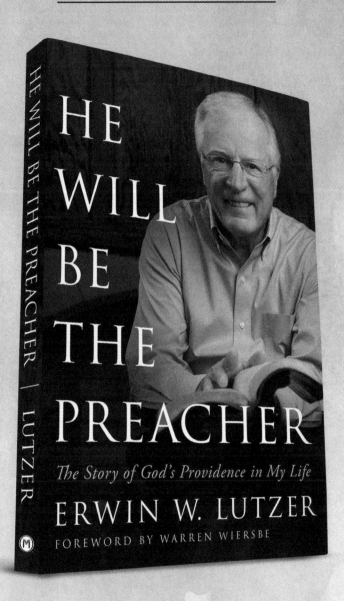

HE WILL BE THE PREACHER | LUTZER

HE WILL BE THE PREACHER

The Story of God's Providence in My Life

ERWIN W. LUTZER

FOREWORD BY WARREN WIERSBE

MOODY Publishers™

From the Word to Life